GHOST
MYSTERIES
UNRAVELING THE WORLD'S MOST
MYSTERIOUS HAUNTINGS

GHOST MYSTERIES

UNRAVELING THE WORLD'S MOST
MYSTERIOUS HAUNTINGS

BY KATHLEEN WEIDNER ZOEHFELD

ILLUSTRATED BY
NATHAN HALE

ALADDIN
NEW YORK   LONDON   TORONTO   SYDNEY

For Scott,
who started asking hard questions when he was three

And for David,
who's always the first one through the door,
notebook and pencil in hand—
and whose ghost stories give me nightmares

◆ ALADDIN

An imprint of Simon & Schuster Children's Publishing Division

1230 Avenue of the Americas, New York, NY 10020

First Simon & Schuster edition August 2009

Text copyright © 2009 by Kathleen Weidner Zoehfeld

Illustrations copyright © 2009 by Nathan Hale

All rights reserved, including the right of reproduction in whole or in part in any form.

ALADDIN is a trademark of Simon & Schuster, Inc., and related logo is a registered trademark of Simon & Schuster, Inc.

Designed by Lisa Vega

The text of this book was set in Adobe Garamond.

For information about special discounts for bulk purchases, please contact Simon & Schuster Special Sales at 1-866-506-1949 or business@simonandschuster.com. The Simon & Schuster Speakers Bureau can bring authors to your live event. For more information or to book an event contact the Simon & Schuster Speakers Bureau at 1-866-248-3049 or visit our website at www.simonspeakers.com.

Manufactured in the United States of America

10 9 8 7 6 5 4 3 2 1

Library of Congress Control Number 2008934662

ISBN 978-1-4169-6448-3

ISBN 978-1-4169-9630-9 (eBook)

CONTENTS

DRIPPING BLOOD AND DRAGGING CHAINS?

While yet a boy I sought for ghosts, and sped
Through many a listening chamber, cave, and ruin,
And starlight wood, with fearful steps pursuing
Hopes of high talk with the departed dead.
—Percy Bysshe Shelley

Are you the kind of person who would love to see a ghost? If you thought a place was haunted, would you be the first person through the door—notebook and pencil in hand, camera ready? Or would you want to run away fast?

For many people, thinking of ghosts conjures up images

of ghoulish forms dripping blood and dragging chains. In horror movies, disturbed mummies plot revenge, and zombies lumber out of their coffins intent on devouring every living creature in their path. In novels and short stories, creepy ghosts like the Bloody Baron and the Headless Horseman may send shivers down your spine. If your first impulse is to *run,* relax. Most people who have reported seeing a ghost say the whole experience was pretty tame.

It's said that every year on All Hallows' Eve—the night of October 31—the spirits of the dead rise up from their graves and wander through the land of the living. But ghost sightings have been reported in all seasons and at all hours of the day and night. Would you know a ghost if you saw one? Most people who believe they've seen a ghost say that, at first, it looked like an ordinary person. But when they tried to get near the ghost, it disappeared like a mist. It may have looked as if it moved through a wall, or it may have vanished into thin air or sunk into the ground.

What *are* these mysterious apparitions? Expert ghost detectives study people's ghost sightings. Over the years, they have investigated thousands upon thousands of ghost reports. Some, of course, are just very good stories told by people who want to entertain or creep out their friends. But some reports come from people who are truly puzzled by what they have seen and heard and felt. Whatever these ghostly appearances are, investigators have noted a few types that seem to happen again and again.

The most common is called a crisis apparition. Many people have experienced this. They see a strange, ghostly image of a friend or relative, only to learn that person has died or been in some kind of serious trouble that day. Sometimes the "ghost" does not appear as an image but only as an eerie or ominous feeling. One schoolteacher reported feeling chilled to the bone while teaching a summer-school class on a hot, muggy day. He put on his suit jacket, but even that didn't help. For a few minutes he still felt cold. When he got home, he received a phone call from a relative, telling him that his twin brother had drowned in a boating accident that day. A crisis apparition happens only once and then is never felt or seen again.

In certain places, many people have seen the same ghost appearing at different times. In this kind of haunting, the spirit of one who has been dead for some time is said to linger, or to be stuck repeating the same activity, in one place. For years, people reported seeing a ghost haunting the Drury Lane Theatre in England. Other ghosts had been spotted in that theater, but this ghost kept returning. It appeared at various times as a soft green glow, a moving blue light, or as a handsome young man the actors nicknamed "The Man in Gray." Whatever it was, something strange was going on in that theater, and many people experienced it.

Sometimes ghosts are thought to lurk around battlefields or other places where awful things have happened. A "phantom soldier" has been spotted wandering around The Little Roundtop in Gettysburg, Pennsylvania. That's the site of a famous Civil War battle. Legend has it that he is looking for his troop and still doesn't know he's been killed. Some people report phantom voices at Gettysburg, and even phantom smells. You often hear it said that ghosts are the souls of people who've suffered some violence in life. But are ghosts mean and violent themselves?

Poltergeists, also known as "noisy ghosts," are about as violent as ghosts get. Poltergeists are heard but never seen, and they don't seem to haunt *places* so much as particular *people*. Wherever that person goes, weird things happen. Rapping or knocking sounds are made, but no source can be found. Vases fly off shelves. Lights flicker on and off. Furniture moves of its own accord. But even with all the objects flying around, people are rarely harmed by poltergeists.

So, are these eerie feelings, misty visions, and strange rappings caused by the spirits of the dead who have somehow slipped back into the world of the living? Are they vivid hallucinations? Or are they mere figments, imagined by people who hope or even expect to see ghosts because of dramatic descriptions they have heard or read about? People have been experiencing ghosts for thousands of years. And people have wondered about them for thousands of years too.

Ghost detectives say that there's not much they can do to prove or disprove a haunting from long ago. But when a new ghost appears or a new haunting begins, they can be a big help. If you are lucky enough to have a chance to investigate a ghost, don't run. Try to pay attention and remember everything you see, hear, and feel. Take pictures. Record any sounds. Write everything down so you don't forget any details. Can you think of any ordinary explanations for your ghostly sighting? A good ghost detective asks good questions and gathers all the evidence!

One of America's most-sighted ghosts is the ghost of Abraham Lincoln. The list of people who have seen or felt Lincoln's presence is long and distinguished. Assassinated in 1865, President Lincoln has been seen haunting the White House in Washington, D.C.; his boyhood home in Springfield, Illinois; and the Ford Theatre, where he was killed. The Lincoln room in the White House is offered as a bedroom to the most honored guests. Many have felt his spirit lingering there. Once when queen Wilhelmina of the Netherlands was visiting President Franklin Roosevelt, she said she woke to

Courtesy of the Library of Congress

a knock at the door. She got up, opened the door, and standing there before her was Abe Lincoln in his familiar beard and top hat. She is said to have fainted right there on the spot.

A religious movement called Spirtualism had become very popular

· CONTINUED ON P. 7 · · ☞

during the Civil War, and Mary Todd Lincoln was an avid Spiritualist and believer in ghosts. So that might be one reason why we see Abe so often. More about that later!

America's most famous poltergeist is the Bell Witch. It's said that around 1817 John Bell, a Tennessee farmer, saw a strange, doglike animal on his land. It was, he said, no earthly animal, because when he shot it, it simply vanished like a mist. As it turns out, the ghostly dog was just an omen of terrible things to come. A few weeks later Bell's house became haunted by a poltergeist that rapped on the walls; moved the furniture; and slapped, pinched, and poked his twelve-year-old daughter, Betsy, in her bed at night. This was a noisy ghost indeed. (It certainly made Betsy scream!)

Late at night the Bells would hear what sounded like the claws of a huge dog scratching on the walls outside. The ghost sometimes shrieked and howled dire warnings of impending doom. When a neighbor asked the ghost to identify itself, it replied, "I am a spirit from everywhere, Heaven, Hell, the Earth. I am in the air, in houses, any place at any time." Later it claimed to be the spirit of a person who had been buried in the nearby woods, whose grave had been dug up and his bones scattered.

One neighbor, Kate Batts, was very angry with Mr. Bell over some business dealings. A few people in town suspected that Kate was a witch and that she was hexing the Bell home, hence the name the Bell Witch.

Poltergeist activities almost always occur in households with teen or preteen daughters. Mischievous—and in Betsy's case, maybe even seriously disturbed—children are usually the focus of such hauntings. More about that later, too!

THE WORLD'S FIRST
GHOST STORIES

All the stories of ghosts and goblins that he had heard . . . now came
crowding upon his recollection. The night grew darker and darker;
the stars seemed to sink deeper in the sky, and driving clouds occasionally hid
them from his sight. He had never felt so lonely and dismal.
He was, moreover, approaching the very place where many of the scenes
of the ghost stories had been laid. . . . —Washington Irving

D o you have a favorite ghost story? Classics such
as Washington Irving's "The Legend of Sleepy
Hollow" or Edgar Allan Poe's "Tell-Tale
Heart" are right up there with the best ghost stories in the
world. Whether or not you believe spirits can come back

to haunt the land of the living, tales like these are creepy and enthralling. And they're really fun. Great authors tell us a lot about human nature and the hopes and fears that are part of everyone's life. If you know a good ghost story, you'll be a big hit as you sit with friends around a campfire or as you gather to tell stories at a party. But did you know that ghost stories are not new? As long as human beings have been telling stories, ghost stories have been among them. People of all times and places have had the same fascination with the world beyond. Some of the oldest stories ever recorded tell of living people interacting with the spirits of the dead.

In ancient Egypt, people built elaborate tombs to ensure that their spirits would be comfortable in the afterlife. The dead were mummified, and their tombs were filled with furniture, clothing, food, and treasures. A rich or important person wanted to make sure he would be well provided for in the afterlife. As far as we know, the first ghost story ever recorded is the tale of Nebusemekh. This nobleman's spirit makes a visit to the high priest of Amun-Re.

The story is carved on limestone tablets from around 1200 BCE. Some of the hieroglyphs have faded or crumbled away over the thousands of years since the story was written. But it's pretty clear that something bad has happened to Nebusemekh's tomb—maybe it's been robbed. That happened a lot in ancient Egypt. The ghost tells the priest that he was a very important person in life. But now he's feeling the wind blowing through the holes in his tomb. He asks the priest to help. The priest promises him a new coffin made of gold and zizyphus wood. (I don't know what zizyphus wood is exactly, but it sounds fancy.)

In spite of the priest's promise, the ghost is very crabby. He has asked four times already, he says, and still nothing's been done. How's he supposed to believe anyone now? The priest tells Nebusemekh he'll give him servants who'll bring holy offerings of water and food every day. The ghost says no! Those things pass and people forget.

What he really wants is good solid stone for his tomb. So the priest sends three servants out to find a safer place to rebuild Nebusemekh's tomb. They return in a good mood. They've found an excellent spot! Beyond that, the ending of the story is lost. I hope the ghost liked the spot, and that he can rest easy for all eternity. After all, we don't want the unhappy mummy of Nebusemekh to come lurching down Main Street any-time soon.

The idea of a ghost being an unquiet soul in search of a proper funeral or a decent burial for his dead body goes way back in history. And stories like it have been told again and again. Nebusemekh's brief story carved on crumbling stone hardly counts as literature, but Homer's *Iliad* is one of the oldest complete epic poems we have. It was written some-time around 800 BCE, and—guess what?—there is a ghost in it! *The Iliad* tells the story of a long war between Greece and Troy. The hero of the story is Achilles, one of the Greek army's greatest warriors.

The Greeks were having a winning streak. They'd just come home from a battle and were dividing up the booty, when Achilles got into a fight with his general, Agamemnon. Achilles had captured a beautiful woman, and he decided he would keep her (this was not a great time in history for women, but *that* is a different story!). Agamemnon liked the way she looked and declared he would be taking her for himself. Achilles argued that he had caught the woman fair and square, so she should be his. Agamemnon harrumphed that he didn't care—he was in charge and he could take whatever he pleased. Achilles retorted that if the general was going to be that way, then he wouldn't fight for him anymore. The general could just see if he'd win any battles without him!

Of course, when Achilles refused to fight, the Greeks started losing battles. Achilles' best friend, Patroclus, tried to convince Achilles to forgive the general. But nothing Patroclus said seemed to make any difference. Then he had a brilliant idea. When the next battle was about to begin, he put on Achilles' famous armor. Both the Greeks and Trojans were fooled. Everyone thought Achilles was back, and the Greeks won the battle. Unfortunately, Patroclus could wear Achilles' armor, but he could not fight like Achilles. Patroclus was killed.

Achilles was heartbroken to lose his best friend. He felt ashamed of himself that he had stayed back, sulking in his tent, while his friend was out fighting in his name. After days of taking bloody revenge against the Trojans who had killed his friend, Achilles was still so upset and angry about Patroclus's death, he had forgotten he needed to get on with the funeral.

Finally, one evening Achilles collapsed exhausted on the shore near the crashing waves. There the ghost of Patroclus appeared to him. The spirit looked just like Patroclus had looked in life, and he wore the same clothes. But he hovered over Achilles' head, moaning in a pitiful way. The ghost urged Achilles to give him a proper funeral soon so he could go to Hades where he now belonged. He reminded Achilles that he too was doomed to die in battle soon.

Achilles reached out to hug his friend one last time, but he vanished just like a mist or vapor, "gibbering and whining into the earth."

Much like the ancient Egyptians, ancient Greeks believed that everyone had a soul or spirit that could go on living after his or her physical body died. If certain funeral ceremonies were not performed, the dead person's soul might start hanging around the world of the living, making a pest of itself. A dead soldier, especially, needed proper funeral services. In ancient Greece a coin would be placed in the dead person's mouth before the funeral. When his spirit arrived at the edge of the river Styx, he could use the coin to pay the boatman, Charon, to get across the river into Hades, the land of the dead. Once he had his coin and his funeral celebrations were complete, the spirit of Patroclus was able to depart.

In Homer's *Odyssey*, the story is the other way around. Instead of a ghost visiting a living person, a living person visits a ghost. Odysseus makes a trek to the dark, mysterious underworld to talk to the spirit of Achilles. Achilles tells Odysseus it's pretty boring being dead. He'd rather be alive as a slave than king of all the dead in Hades.

Some ghost stories are so vivid and have been told for so long, people wonder if they are actual records of real events or just very good stories. The ancient Chinese philosopher, Mozi, lived between 470 and 391 BCE. He may have been one of the world's first ghost investigators. Many ghost stories, he warned, could not be trusted. Everybody has his or her own story, which no one else has witnessed. Since the stories vary, and the experiences they describe can't be repeated, how can you be sure? In spite of that, he believed that *some* ghost reports simply could not be refuted.

According to a famous Chinese legend, around 800 BCE, King Xuan of Zhou trumped up false charges against his minister, Du Bo, and ordered him to be executed. Du Bo declared he was innocent. If his spirit was able to go on after life, he said, he would return to seek revenge for his unjust death. The king went ahead with the execution anyway.

Three years later, the legend says, King Xuan called for a meeting of all his feudal lords. As people gathered for the big event, Du Bo's ghost appeared driving a plain chariot pulled by a white horse. The ghost was robed in red and carried a red bow and arrows. Slowly, deliberately, the spirit approached the king, lifted his bow, and took aim. The red arrow went straight through the king's heart, killing him on the spot.

Everyone knew this story, and Mozi wondered if it was true. Because a whole assembly of feudal lords had witnessed the murder, and because they all reported seeing the same thing, Mozi concluded that the story was convincing. "As we are to rely on what many have jointly seen and what many have jointly heard, the case of Du Bo," he concluded, "is to be accepted."

Some ghost detectives use this philosophy today. But there is a flaw in Mozi's logic. Who's to say that the feudal lords themselves didn't stage the murder to avenge Du Bo? Or maybe someone murdered the king in front of the lords, using clever devices to make the lords *think* they had seen a ghost. Just because a lot of people saw *something* does not prove that that something was a spirit. There are plenty of ways even large groups of people can be fooled.

Still, the story of Du Bo was important. It told people that murdering an innocent person was not okay—even if you were a king. It reminded people that the past did not simply vanish, that the dead remember us and we remember them. If necessary, ghosts can return to Earth to punish the evil or to reward the just.

The first classic ghost story—one that we might tell around a campfire today—was written sometime around

100 CE. This story comes from ancient Rome. Pliny the Younger was a famous philosopher, judge, and writer. He is best known for his many letters to friends about daily life and politics in Rome. One of those letters isn't about politics, though—it's about a mysterious house in Athens. Pliny writes to his friend, Lucius Licinius Sura, asking him whether he believes in the existence of ghosts.

He tells Sura that a very trustworthy man has told him about a strange house. It was a large and roomy house, but no one wanted to live there. Everyone who had tried had the same horrifying story to tell. They said that late at night, they'd be awakened by the sound of chains clanking. As they lay in bed shivering in fear, the clanking sounds would move closer and closer. If they dared peek out from under their blankets, they would see the misty phantom of a skinny old man with a long beard and wild hair looming over their bed. If they tried to close their eyes and ignore him, they would hear him moaning. Even louder and more terrifying would be the sound of the rattling chains, which were manacled to his wrists and ankles.

After many sleepless nights, they would begin to feel

very jumpy. It didn't take much more before they would be truly crazed. It was no use being brave and trying to deny the existence of the ghost. Those who'd been foolish enough to stay on in spite of the haunting were said to have died from the stress.

Eventually, everyone abandoned the house to the ghost. The landlord's only hope was that a stranger might come to town and rent the house before he'd heard anything about the haunting. The landlord posted a FOR RENT sign.

The philosopher Athenodoros Cananites came to Athens at that time, and he needed a place to stay. He saw the sign and asked about the price. "Cheap!" cried the landlord. The price was *so* cheap, Athenodoros became suspicious. He asked the locals if they knew anything about the house. Everyone told the same scary story. Far from being frightened, the philosopher was intrigued. He told the landlord he'd take it!

On the first evening in his new house, Athenodoros ordered his servants to set up a couch for him in the front part of the house. When everyone else had gone to bed, Athenodoros lit the lamp beside his couch and gathered his pencils and writing tablets. He would keep busy with his writing, and those imaginary noises would stay away.

Hours went by, and the house was completely silent. Then, Athenodoros began to hear strange, faraway clanking noises. He kept at his work and tried to ignore the sounds. Surely they were just ordinary sounds. But gradually they grew louder and closer until it seemed as if they were right there in the room with him. He looked up, and there was the thin, misty, wild-haired ghost the locals had described. The ghost beckoned the philosopher to follow him.

Trying to remain calm, Athenodoros lifted his hand and motioned to the ghost to wait. He put his pencil to the tablet and went on writing, hoping this was just a hallucination that would soon disappear. The ghost rattled his chains over the philosopher's head and beckoned even more urgently. There could be no ignoring him. Athenodoros braced himself and picked up his lamp. He nodded to the ghost that he would follow. The ghost shuffled slowly to the courtyard, as if weighed down by the chains on his ankles. Then, suddenly, he vanished before Athenodoros's eyes.

Thinking quickly, the philosopher made a small pile of

grass and leaves at exactly the spot where the ghost had disappeared. The next morning he called the police and asked them to dig in that spot. When the earth had been shoveled away, they discovered the skeleton of a man in chains. Once the bones were buried in a graveyard and all the proper funeral ceremonies had been performed, the house was haunted no more.

Nearly two thousand years have gone by since Pliny the Younger wrote about Athenodoros and the man in chains. To this day people all around the world tell stories of haunted places. Those stories have many similarities. They start with a series of weird events. Fear and puzzlement grow in the hearts and minds of witnesses. They try to remain calm and investigate all the clues. They are surprised and terrified by even stranger happenings. The story reaches its climax with the revelation of a tortured soul who has come back to Earth to right a wrong or to bring a warning or important message to a loved one. We almost always root for the ghost, even if he or she might seem scary or creepy or dangerous. The ghost is the ultimate underdog—the classic poor, wronged soul with obstacles to overcome before justice can be attained.

It's hard to imagine a bigger obstacle than being dead. Once the ghost is able to get someone to listen to his message, once the wrong can be righted, the ghost can relax and make his journey to the other world where he belongs.

Ghost stories can be entertaining and even instructional. But do they prove that real spirits can come back from the dead? Most of them happened so long ago, there is no chance that they could ever be investigated now in any satisfying way. Even if, as in Mozi's story, many people said they witnessed the same ghost, there is no way to verify if what those people saw was a ghost or something else. For the most part, good ghost stories are simply good literature. They tell us more about the living than the dead.

But, you ask, are at least *some* of those stories true? If you were Lucius Licinius Sura, what would you have written in your letter back to your friend Pliny? Do you believe in the existence of ghosts? One modern British philosopher, who sometimes wrote articles for the Society for Psychical Research, complained about that question. He said it was a silly question. A better one, he said, would be: "Do you believe that people sometimes experience apparitions?" To that question, he answered, yes. "No one," he said, "who examines the evidence can come to any other conclusion. Instead of disputing the facts, we must try to explain them!"

Countless stories of famous hauntings have this classic man-in-chains ending. Remember the haunted Drury Lane Theatre and the Man in Gray? As that story goes, when the theater was renovated, workmen were horrified to discover a skeleton, dressed in a tattered gray riding coat, with a knife in its ribs. Once the skeleton was buried, they say, the haunting stopped.

HOW TO HAUNT
YOUR OWN HOUSE

For truth is always strange; stranger than fiction.
—George Gordon Byron

In stories, authors get to make up all sorts of weird stuff. But real life can be much stranger. People are sometimes troubled—even terrified—by mysterious sightings and events they can't explain. And it's not only in their homes. Hair-raising happenings have been reported in churches, hotels, theaters, graveyards, castles, jails, schools, restaurants, and even aboard airplanes—just about anyplace you can imagine. Is there a place near you that everyone says is haunted? Is the haunting driving everyone crazy or frightening them away? If so, it may be time to call in a ghost investigator. Ghost investigators try to get to the bottom of these things so people can go on with their lives in peace. In most cases, perfectly ordinary causes are discovered, but sometimes rooting out the truth can take a lot of detective work.

In spite of thousands of years of hauntings, the job of ghost investigator is a relatively recent one. One of the pioneers in the field was a man named Harry Price. He was independently wealthy and a leader in England's Society for Psychical Research. He's probably best known for his fifteen-year study of the Borley Rectory, which he called "the most haunted house in England." If you think fifteen years seems like a long time to  spend studying a haunted house, you may be right. Some people have suggested that, in this case, the ghost detective might have been doing a little of the haunting himself.

It all started in 1863 when the Reverend Henry Bull ordered a rectory to be built near his church in Essex County, about sixty miles north of London. Photos of the house show that it was a staid, austere-looking brick structure. After Henry Bull died, his son, Harry Bull, and his family lived there, serving the church for many more years. After Harry passed away, the house stood empty for a while. And that's when the problems began.

Over the years, the local people had come to believe the house was haunted. Now they made a point of staying away from it, especially after dark. Perhaps the colorful stories that Harry Bull and his four sisters had been fond of telling

had fueled the local legend. When they were young girls, Harry's sisters said they saw the ghost of a nun drifting over one of the paths in their garden. They named the path "the nun's walk." That was just the beginning. The strange sightings went on for years. Folks remembered young Harry Bull telling the story of how he saw a phantom coach pulled by ghost horses, being driven down the "nun's path" by two headless ghouls.

The story was repeated again and again. According to everyone's favorite version, the Borley Rectory had been built on the site of a medieval monastery. Long, long ago, a nun from a nearby convent fell in love with one of the Borley monks. The couple, with the help of a friend, tried to run away together to be married. As they were fleeing down the road in a horse and carriage, they were caught. Their punishment was harsh, to say the least. The abbot ordered the monk and his friend to be hanged, and the nun was bricked up alive inside one of the walls of the monastery. Since that time, the ghost of the nun could be seen haunting the place—usually at dusk or after dark, but sometimes even in broad daylight.

The Essex church elders asked several clergyman and their families to come and replace the departed Rev. Harry Bull. Knowing the legend that surrounded the rectory, many ministers refused. Finally, in 1928, the Reverend G. E. Smith and his wife accepted. They said they did not believe in ghosts.

Not long after the Smiths moved in, a local newspaper ran a few articles about the legendary haunting. Harry Price read the articles with great interest. On June 12, 1929, he decided to pay the Smiths a visit at the Borley Rectory. The Smiths told Price that some weird things had indeed happened since they moved in. Every once in a while they would hear the sound of footsteps, even when they were sure no one else could possibly be around. They heard strange whispers and, from time to time, saw a mysterious light in the windows in a part of the house they never used. Two of their maids believed they had seen the ghost of the nun. And the Reverend Smith said he had once seen a strange, misty column swirling up outside in the garden. Price asked the Smiths if he could investigate the house, and they agreed. They hoped that the great ghost researcher from the psychic society would help calm people's irrational fears of the place.

They must have been quite impressed when he arrived equipped with still and movie cameras, notebooks, drawing pads, measuring tapes, chalk, string, and a vial of mercury for detecting the slightest of vibrations. As soon as he got there, though, weird things began to happen. Without anyone touching them, bells rang and furniture moved. Small objects flew across the room. Price took photos and movies of the events. He drew chalk circles around pieces of furniture so that he would be able to measure exactly how far they had been transported.

He interviewed the hired help and took detailed notes. After he had talked to each of them, Price had a long list of poltergeist problems that they said had happened again and again in the rectory, over the course of many years: moving furniture, smashed dishes, banging doors, strange voices, footsteps, mysterious writing on the walls, sudden changes in temperature, ethereal music, strange lights, the sound of galloping horses, phantom odors, rappings. . . . Parts of the house had been even known to burst spontaneously into flames!

On July 15, 1929, the Smiths moved out of the Borley Rectory. A reporter jokingly asked them if the ghosts had finally chased them away. They laughed and said no, they still did not believe in ghosts. The house was just uncomfortable and the water and plumbing were bad.

The Borley Rectory sat empty again for many months. Then on October 16, 1930, the Reverend Lionel Algernon Foyster and his wife, Marianne Foyster, moved in. The Reverend Foyster was a cousin of the Bulls. After the Foysters had lived in the rectory for a year, Price received a letter. It was from two of the Bull sisters. They said that their cousin and his wife were being troubled by poltergeists. They begged him to come back and continue his investigations.

On the night Price arrived, the butler filled the guests' glasses with wine, and it turned into ink before their eyes. Marianne sighed in frustration, claiming that she had been simply overwhelmed with poltergeist troubles. Her three-year-old daughter had been locked inside a room all by herself, and the key had vanished. Their best dishes had fallen off shelves and shattered. But scariest of all were the mysterious words that kept appearing on the walls—creepy messages addressed to Marianne herself. At dinner she told Price that she hated the Borley Rectory and longed to move away.

Since the mischief seemed to happen only when Marianne was around, Price suggested that maybe she was the focus of all the trouble. Still, he did not accuse her of writing on the walls herself. Maybe, he said, the terrible tale of

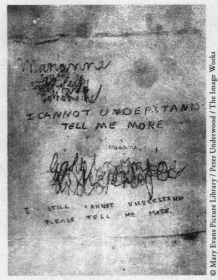

© Mary Evans Picture Library / Peter Underwood / The Image Works

the trapped nun was true. Maybe the nun hoped Marianne would be someone she could finally talk to.

In 1935 Marianne and her husband moved away from the gloomy brick house. Saying that he was determined to figure out the mystery, Price rented the place himself in

1937, and he and a friend began to stay there overnight from time to time. When they did, they heard odd thumps, and they woke to find various pieces of furniture moved outside their chalk circles. Price put a want ad in the newspaper asking for more assistants:

> HAUNTED HOUSE: Responsible persons of leisure and intelligence, intrepid, critical, and unbiased, are invited to join rota of observers in a year's night and day investigation of alleged haunted house in Home counties. Printed Instructions supplied. Scientific training or ability to operate simple instruments an advantage. House situated in lonely hamlet, so own car is essential. Write Box H.989, The Times, E.C.4

Two hundred people applied. Price and his friend hired forty. A few were amateur spiritual mediums—people who were said to have special talents in contacting and communicating with the dead.

Through one of the mediums, Price said, they learned more about the nun's story. For some reason, this version did not include a monastery and a cruel abbot. A spirit who called herself Marie Lairre said that she had been a nun in a French convent. She'd been enticed to England by a prominent member of a Catholic family, who had asked her to run away from the convent and marry him. Once in Borley, though, things were not exactly lovey-dovey for the new couple. Marie's fiancé ended up strangling her in one of the barns. She said her body had been buried beneath the cellar floor of the house. It was pretty clear to Price that she would haunt the place until they found her bones and gave her a decent Christian burial.

On March 27, 1938, one of Price's mediums, using a device something like a Ouija board, received an ominous message. The spirit said that a mysterious person named "Sunex Amures" and one of his men would start a fire that night over the hall, and the rectory would burn to the ground. The burning would end the haunting and finally reveal the whole truth about the murdered nun. Price and his assistants watched nervously that night. But there was no fire, and the rectory was still standing the next morning.

In spite of all Price's impressive paraphernalia, his large

crew of assistants, and his professional manner—he did not seem to favor, and in most cases did not even report, the possibility of the simplest explanations for the mysterious events: that the "footsteps" could have been caused by old water pipes or rats and mice scampering in the walls. That the whispering voices could have been the voices of people walking by outside, amplified by the odd acoustics of the house itself. That the mist the Reverend Smith had seen in the garden was not a ghost but, as Smith himself later concluded, just a plume of smoke. And those weird lights in the windows? With a little further observation, Smith realized they were simply reflections on the glass from the lights of trains passing in the distance.

What about the flying objects? Was the angry ex-nun rearranging the furniture and throwing vases? If she could move a couch, why didn't she just show Price where she was buried? A newspaper reporter said that one night he was helping Price with his investigations in the rectory, when he was conked in the head by a flying object. Suspicious, he tackled the respected researcher—and found his pockets full of small stones. Unless Price's stash of rocks was meant to fend off the poor nun, at least some of the Borley Rectory's poltergeist activity must have been perpetrated by the great investigator himself. Maybe Price figured as long as he could keep the mysterious shenanigans going, people would stay interested, and he would still have a job—*and* a lot of attention. Or, as his personal secretary once declared, perhaps he was just the kind of person who attracted ghosts.

The Smiths had hoped that Price would help calm people's fears. But instead the locals were even more scared than before, and thanks to Price, the house's reputation for being haunted spread all around the globe.

In 1938 historians proved that there had never been a monastery in Borley. There was absolutely no historical basis for the medieval legend of the monk and the nun. Still Price forged on with his investigations, now equipped with the new story of the British man luring the French nun to her doom.

Less than a year after the ominous fire prediction, the Borley Rectory did burn down. But there was no "Sunex Amures" and no ghost. The man who lived in the house at that time, Captain William H. Gregson, accidentally knocked over an oil lamp in the hallway, and the fire spread quickly.

Price went on studying the place until the burned-out rectory was torn down completely in 1944, announcing to the press at one point that he had found bones in the cellar. Later, members of the Society of Psychical Research were very critical of Price's sometimes haphazard and always showy methods of investigating the Borley Rectory. Price claimed that his investigations only uncovered deeper and deeper mysteries. Was the great Harry Price really baffled by deep mysteries? Or was he just fooling everyone?

Back then, thousands of people read Price's ghost reports. They read with wide, wondering eyes and great gasps of amazement. Today not many people still believe that the weird happenings Price observed and recorded were actually the work of ghosts. We can only hope that ghost detectives today, no matter how much they may admire Price and his pioneer investigations, do not try to follow *exactly* in his footsteps. Most ghost investigators are not deliberately trying to fool the people they are supposed to be helping. But there are always a few who will try to fool others, no matter when or where.

In December 1975 the Lutz family was hunting for a new home in New York. They were having a lot of trouble finding the right house. It looked as if a house big enough to hold their family of five—two parents and three children—would be way too expensive for them. Then one day their real-estate agent showed them a house that felt like a mansion to them. It was in Amityville, Long Island—exactly where they wanted to be. It had six bedrooms, a swimming pool, and a nice boathouse on the river nearby. Kathleen Lutz loved the place, but she hardly dared ask the price. Her real-estate agent said they could get it cheap. When Mrs. Lutz asked the agent how on earth the price could be so low, the agent told her that the house had been the site of a gruesome mass murder. People were terrified of the place.

On November 13, 1974, a twenty-three-year-old named Ronald DeFeo shot and killed his mother, father, and four younger siblings in that house. This was not a made-up legend from long ago. This murder really did happen.

And it had happened only the year before. Like everyone else in the nation, the Lutzes were horrified by the crime, but they said they were not superstitious. A house was just a house. And they decided to take the deal. Just in case, they had the house blessed by a local priest before they moved in.

As it turns out, the Lutz family lived in the house for only one month before they packed up their things and ran away in terror!

In 1977 author Jay Anson published a book called *The Amityville Horror*. He said it was an accurate description of the Lutzes' weird experiences once they moved into their new home. The Lutzes told him that they soon began to see ghostly apparitions. Dark-hooded figures appeared to them at night.

They told Anson about strange, unearthly voices that seemed to spring out from inside them. Kathleen Lutz said that once she had been lifted off her feet by an invisible force and set down in front of a closet. Inside that closet she and her husband, George, discovered a dark passageway to a secret room. Its walls, floor, and ceiling were painted bloodred. What that room might have been used for, she said, they were afraid to even imagine.

They described scenes of terrifying poltergeist activities. Swarms of flies attacked the children in their playroom, even though it was the dead of winter. Green slippery slime appeared, dangerously, on the stairs. Small objects floated in midair. Windows cracked. The temperature in a room would sometimes change dramatically for no reason at all. At times they could hear the muffled music of a marching band, but they had no idea where it could be coming from. Worst of all, their five-year-old daughter, Missy, began talking to an evil spirit pig named "Jodie."

George Lutz grew a beard, and the kids were even more creeped out. They thought their father was beginning to take on an eerie resemblance to Ronald, the murderer. They became so frightened; they felt sick and couldn't go to school. Mr. Lutz said he was so overwhelmed by the whole ordeal he couldn't rest and he couldn't work. Mr. and Mrs. Lutz said that the priest who had come to bless the house had gotten desperately ill as well.

Mr. Lutz called in investigators from the Psychical

Research Foundation and the American Society for Psychical Research. Like everyone else in the nation, they had read the supposedly true-life story of the Amityville haunting. But, after investigating the house, the researchers were skeptical. They said they found no evidence of any ghostly haunting. Skeptics pointed out many errors in the book, too. The book described terrible, treacherous weather during the Lutzs' four-week trauma. The real weather records show that, actually, the weather was pretty nice for January in New York.

The book told of a creepy legend about an ancient well, deep under the foundation of the house. There, it was said, Native Americans used to place sick and insane members of their tribe until they died of exposure to the elements. After a little bit of research, the investigators found that this story was completely made up.

A few years later, Ronald DeFeo's lawyer surprised everyone with a confession. He said that he and Kathleen and George Lutz had cooked up the whole story of the haunting over dinner one night. They had planned how they would get the story published and how they would get movie rights for the story too. The lawyer, William Weber, was miffed at the Lutzes because they had taken all the profits from the book and hadn't shared any with him. The priest sued them all for saying things about him that weren't true. He said that he hadn't gotten sick at all.

This time it wasn't the ghost investigator who was fooling everyone—it was the people who claimed they were being haunted. Luckily, honest investigators have been able to figure out the real causes of most hauntings. Of course, there are a few that remain mysterious. Does that mean those places are, or were, in fact, haunted? Or does it just mean we haven't yet figured out the reason for those particular events?

How you answer will tell you something about

Harry Price carried chalk and string and measuring tapes. What would be in a ghost investigator's high-tech toolbox today? In the hit Syfy Channel TV show *Ghost Hunters,* the stars, Jason Hawes and Grant Wilson, use all kinds of fancy electronic equipment to help them detect "paranormal activity"—digital thermometers, EMF (electromagnetic field) scanners, infrared and night-vision cameras, handheld digital video cameras, digital audio recorders, and laptop computers. Their ion generator (a machine that puts an

• • • • • • • • CONTINUED ON P. 42 • • ☞

electrical charge in the surrounding air) and white noise generator (which creates a soft, steady, static noise) are set up, they say, to help spirit entities who want to make themselves seen or heard. Most of this paraphernalia has little to do with figuring out what is making strange things happen in any given place—it just makes a more exciting and dramatic show.

Surprisingly, doing a real ghost investigation does not take any complicated equipment at all. It's not a whole lot different from what Price needed one hundred years ago (minus, one would hope, the pocket full of stones!). Expert real-life ghost investigator Benjamin Radford says he usually needs no more than a camera, a small notebook, and a tape recorder. Of course he is looking for *normal* activities, not paranormal ones.

yourself. What's your rating on the scale of skepticism? But, wait! Before you answer, first sit back and read about the story of a haunted house that began a whole new religious movement.

The *Flying Dutchman* was a merchant ship built in the 1600s. Legend says that the *Flying Dutchman* was cursed when its Dutch captain refused to sail into a safe harbor during a terrible storm. The crew begged their captain to do the right thing, but he just shook his fist at

• CONTINUED ON P. 43 • •

God and dared him to take them down. This ghost ship has haunted the high seas ever since.

When sailors see a hazy image or strange light on the horizon, they say it's the *Flying Dutchman*—an omen of bad luck or doom. If you love the Pirates of the Caribbean movies, you know about this ghost ship!

STRANGE RAPS IN
THE NIGHT

An idea, like a ghost, must be spoken to a little before it will explain itself.
—Charles Dickens

Have you ever played a trick just to annoy your parents? That's what Maggie Fox did when she was fifteen years old. You know how you feel when you've done something mean or sneaky or wrong and you're terrified your mom will find out? What do you do? Well, you could try to hide it. You could tell a lie and then another lie and then another and another and try to keep her guessing. But you know what you *should* do. 'Fess up! Come clean! That is the best advice. The *only* advice! Take your punishment and get it over with. Do not be like Maggie and her little sister, who were too afraid to tell the truth. They had to keep repeating the trick for everyone—not only for their mother—but in front of the whole world for . . . are you sitting down? For *forty* years! Their poor old mother never did learn the truth.

Here's how it all happened. It was 1847, and Maggie and her ten-year-old sister, Kate, and their mom and dad were living in Rochester, New York. Maggie loved the big city. She loved to listen to the *clip-clop* of the horses pulling their stagecoaches and wagons past her bedroom window late at night. She loved the shops full of lovely perfumes and laces, fancy hats, and jewelry. She loved the market and the bakeries, where they could buy all kinds of delicious food. And she enjoyed the interesting visitors who stopped by nearly every day—people who knew her older sister, Leah, who gave piano lessons to the children of Rochester's more well-to-do residents. Leah had a daughter named Lizzie, who was about Maggie's age. The girls enjoyed exploring the shops and hanging out together.

Maggie's parents weren't so fond of the city. They were getting older, and what they wanted more than anything else was a quiet life in the country. John Fox applied for a job as blacksmith in the little town of Hydesville, New York. When he got the job, he and his wife, Margaret, were very happy. Two of their older, married children owned farms near Hydesville. Mrs. Fox liked the idea of having them nearby. So, in the middle of December, just two weeks before Christmas, the Fox family packed up their things, loaded them into a wagon, and headed off through the snow to their new house. It was a small, square wooden house with a big front parlor, a kitchen, one bedroom, a cellar below, and an attic up above.

Maggie was mad. Her parents had dragged her to this little farmhouse in the middle of nowhere. Day after day the skies were gray, and all it did was snow, snow, snow. Nobody ever visited, and there wasn't a thing to do. She glowered at her simple, stick-in-the-mud parents and told them she was bored. Her mom suggested that there were plenty of household chores to keep her busy. Argh! Maggie could have screamed!

Then, late one night in March 1848, when Maggie was lying in bed listening to the quiet of the still-snowbound countryside and missing the constant hubbub and traffic of the city, she heard a strange sound. It sounded like clopping hooves! Or, wait a minute . . . now it sounded like footsteps. No, it was more of a knocking or rapping sound. Her mom and dad were asleep. Could there be someone else in the house? Was a burglar trying to get in?

Before long, the knocking woke up Mrs. Fox. She sprang out of bed, lit a candle, and began searching the house.

In the bed next to her, Maggie thought she heard her sister Kate stifle a giggle. *Hmmm,* she thought. *What is that little mischief maker up to?*

The rapping continued. Terrified, Margaret shook her husband awake. Try as they might, Margaret and John could not figure out where the sound was coming from.

Of course, Maggie suspected her sister, but she decided to keep quiet about it. The next morning, she grilled Kate. Only too delighted to explain her prank, Kate pulled up the bedcovers and showed Maggie the apple she was hiding. She had tied a long string to it. Once everyone had fallen asleep, she said, she dangled the apple down and thumped it on the floor. "Like this!" She demonstrated. *Thump, thump, thump.*

But Kate had something even cooler to show Maggie. "Watch!" she said, pointing to her bare foot. Kate moved one toe against another, and her toe joint made the most amazing sound. Maggie could not believe what a big sound her sister's little toe could make. When Kate pressed her foot against the foot of the bed or against the floorboards, the sound was even bigger! Within minutes, Kate taught Maggie how to rap her toes too.

Night after night, the energetic girls made their rapping, tapping noises. Night after night Mr. and Mrs. Fox lay awake quaking in fear. Night after night they searched. They searched the cellar and they searched the attic. They searched inside and they searched outside. Still they could not figure out the reason for the knocks. Maggie and Kate had to bury their faces in their pillows to muffle their giggles. Their old mom and dad looked so comical in their nightcaps and pajamas, hopelessly searching the house.

After several nights without sleep, their parents were exhausted, and their mom was sick with worry. By March 31—April Fool's Day eve—Mrs. Fox decided that they'd had enough. They would all go to bed and no matter what happened, no matter how much knocking and rapping went on, they would ignore it. They would sleep. It would go away.

But it didn't. That night something really strange happened. When the mysterious rapping began, Kate snapped her fingers in reply. Much to her mom's astonishment, the raps began to mimic Kate's finger snappings exactly. If Kate snapped three, the raps rapped three back. It was eerie. Was someone trying to communicate with them? The raps seemed to be driven by some intelligent force.

Maggie joined in her sister's game. "Now do this just as I do," she commanded. "Count one, two, three, four." She struck her palm four times with her fist. Four raps replied—seemingly out of nowhere.

Maggie gasped in fake astonishment.

"Count to ten," said Mrs. Fox.

Ten raps rapped back.

Mrs. Fox tried something a little more difficult. "How old is Maggie?" she asked.

Fifteen raps came in reply. Maggie had just celebrated her fifteenth birthday. Now Mrs. Fox was sure she was talking to a *someone*—a being who could see them and know them.

"If you are a spirit, knock twice," cried Mrs. Fox.

Two raps sounded almost immediately.

Mrs. Fox questioned the spirit further and found out that he had been badly injured in their house. In fact, not only was he injured, he had been *killed* in their house!

Kate and Maggie clung to each other trembling and crying in horror at the gruesome tale. (Which, of course, they themselves were making up.) Maybe they were also feeling a little scared by how perfectly their trick was working!

Even though it was eight o'clock at night, Mrs. Fox rushed out and called in the neighbors as witnesses. Before long more than a dozen people had squeezed into the little house. One of the neighbors took over the job of questioning the spirit, and he soon figured out that the spirit "was murdered in the bedroom about five years ago, and that the murder was committed by a Mr. John Bell, on a Tuesday night at 12 o'clock; that it was murdered by having its throat cut with a butcher knife; that the body was taken down to the cellar, and that it was not buried until the next night; and that it was buried ten feet below the surface of the ground."

The spirit went on to tell the guests that he had been a wandering peddler. Business had been good. He'd managed to save five hundred dollars. He was carrying it around with him in one of his tin boxes when he called on the Bell family, who lived in the house at the time. He said that he sold Mrs. Bell a few items, but when Mr. Bell got a glimpse of all that money, he decided to steal it.

The peddler's story spread fast. The next day hundreds of people flocked to the house from miles around. There were so many, they had to take turns going in, so everyone would get a chance to hear the weird sounds. No longer would Maggie have to fret that they didn't have any visitors. Local newspapers were soon running headline stories about the "Ghost of Hydesville"! And everyone had to see or hear it for themselves.

Mr. Fox and a team of men tried to dig up the dead body in the cellar. But they had dug only a few feet down when they hit an underground stream and couldn't go any deeper.

The peddler's tale astonished Mrs. Fox and many of the neighbors. But it was a story that would have been easy for the girls to invent. Back then, people in small towns had no malls or big stores nearby. When they needed a simple household item, they had to rely on peddlers who went door to door. Peddlers led rootless lives. You might buy an eggbeater from a peddler one day and then not see him again for months. He would be busy traveling to other towns. A peddler-gone-missing was a favorite subject of local

Courtesy of the Library of Congress

folklore—and of creepy ghost stories kids liked to make up on their own!

Newspaper reporters interviewed other people who had lived in the Hydesville house. Some of them said that they, too, had heard odd knocks and noises. A teenage maid who used to work for the Bell family told a reporter she did remember a peddler who came and stayed overnight at the house. That day, the Bells sent her to her parents' house for a week. When she returned, Mrs. Bell was using new needles and expensive silver thimbles for her sewing, but the peddler was . . . gone! (Of *course* the peddler was gone. Duh!)

The maid said Mrs. Bell sent her to the dark, musty cellar on an errand. As soon as she got down the stairs, her feet sank into loose dirt on the floor. She said she felt scared in the dark with her feet stuck in the dirt. Mrs. Bell told her that rats had been digging holes in the cellar, and Mr. Bell was trying to get them filled in with dirt. Rats were bad enough, but the maid suspected the dirt might be a sign of something far worse. Was he trying to cover up an unspeakable deed? Was there a dead body in the basement of the house at Hydesville?

At this time, Mr. Bell and his family lived in another town a few miles away. Shocked by the preposterous story running in the local newspapers, Mr. Bell (no relation to the other unfortunate Mr. Bell who was plagued by the "Bell Witch") claimed he was innocent. Mrs. Bell said the peddler she had bought the thimbles from was alive and well and had been back several times. Sad to say, the Bell's friends and neighbors—although they insisted they believed Mr. and Mrs. Bell—began to avoid them like the plague.

Back at the house in Hydesville, most of the visitors

had quickly gotten over the tale of the slaughtered peddler. They had moved on to better things. Through Maggie and Kate, they were now able to talk to the spirits of their dead loved ones. Night after night, people came, hoping to hear what important words their dear ghosts might have for them. Many went away convinced that they had received special messages from the world beyond.

Poor Mrs. Fox was exhausted by all the excitement. She packed up her family and they ran away from the noisy house. Mr. and Mrs. Fox took shelter with one of their married children and his family. But much to Mrs. Fox's surprise, the rappings were not left behind in the haunted house. They seemed to follow Maggie and Kate—especially Kate—wherever the children went. Mrs. Fox became convinced that her youngest children were channeling spirits. If she and Mr. Fox were ever going to get the quiet life they longed for, they realized they'd have to send their daughters back to Rochester to live with Leah.

As soon as the girls arrived in the big city, Leah loomed over them sternly and commanded them to show her exactly how they did their trick. Or else! She said she would tell their mother what they were up to, and they'd be sent back to Hydesville to be punished without further ado. The girls were trapped. Caught!

They explained the whole prank to Leah, and she was thrilled. Unfortunately she now had her hands full trying to control the "poltergeist" activity that seemed to happen wherever the rambunctious girls went. She discovered the best way to keep them under control was to keep them busy.

Leah invited in the neighbors—but only a few carefully chosen people at a time. She would ask them to sit around a table in the parlor. The oil lamps were turned down low. Everyone would place their hands on top of the table, their fingers touching the fingers of the people on either side. Leah would lead the guests in a few prayers. Then she would play soft music on the piano to get them in the right mood. Usually Kate acted as the medium, or the go-between. Mediums—like those employed later by Harry Price so he could talk to the ghost of the Borley Rectory—are people who say they can allow themselves to be possessed by spirits of the dead so that those spirits can converse with the living. The idea of medium-ship was not new, but the role of medium as we know it today began with Kate Fox at the table in her big sister's parlor.

Kate would go into a trance. The guests would sit quietly alert, breathless, waiting for the first knock—the sign that a spirit was with them. Soon a soft rap or two would announce the spirit's full presence. Then the guests could begin questioning it.

At some point, Leah would ask the guests to pull their chairs away from the table, place their feet on the rungs of their chairs, and raise their hands in the air. Much to everyone's amazement, the heavy table would then slide across the floor as easily as if a grown man had been pushing it. But no person appeared to be touching it at all. No *mortal* person that is! Leah told them that as long as Kate was present, the spirits could come from the spirit world into the physical world, where they could move things (or throw things if they were feeling cranky).

These small gatherings where people sit around a table holding hands are called séances. People had held séances before the Fox sisters' time, but only a few. In all the old ghost stories, when a spirit returned to the world of the living, it was almost always with an urgent task in mind—some terrible wrong that needed to be made right—or with a vital message or dire warning for a special loved one. Now, apparently, ghosts could come just to chat.

Leah's Rochester séances soon became very popular. One evening her daughter, Lizzie, said she wished the spirits would go away before someone got hurt or her mother and young aunts got labeled as frauds. Leah angrily declared that Lizzie had "offended the spirits." She sent Lizzie away to live with her father in Indiana.

Leah put her managerial skills to work, and by November 1849, Kate and Maggie found themselves communicating with ghosts for a sell-out crowd at one of Rochester's biggest, fanciest auditoriums. The girls—with their innocent, almost ethereal beauty and hair as black as ravens' wings—were described in all the newspapers. Over the next few years, they performed for large crowds in many cities. All across America, people were entranced. They wanted to hold séances too!

Before long there were not hundreds, but millions of people in the United States who considered themselves devout followers. The Spiritualist movement had been born! Some of the new Spiritualists began to discover their talents as mediums too. Soon the craze spread across the Atlantic Ocean to Europe. Spiritualist mediums had a few critics who tried to denounce them as frauds, but the Spiritualists had far more loyal followers. Many of their devotees were wealthy citizens with powerful positions in society.

What did traditional religious leaders have to say about the Spiritualist movement when it began? Many were suspicious about the whole idea of people trying to contact ghosts and spirits. Maybe it's because priests and ministers and rabbis know how easy it can be for someone to take advantage of those who have lost loved ones. People who are lonely and grieving can be very vulnerable. And there were certainly *lots* of grieving people around in Maggie and Kate's time. In the mid-1800s one out of three children died before they ever reached adulthood. That means that nearly every family had watched at least one child die. Scientists back then were still trying to figure out how to stop awful diseases like typhus, cholera, yellow fever, and polio from claiming the lives of so many.

If you are ever tempted to think that the grown-ups in your life do not care about you, listen up. They care. Moms, dads, uncles, aunts, grandparents, godparents, foster parents, teachers—they all care. They may be busy. They may be stressed and grumpy. But they care. If you were gone, all they would want in the world would be to know that you are okay. If it were possible to know that the kindly spirits of great-grandparents were watching over you in Heaven . . . well, they would give anything to be assured of that. Grown-ups who lose children are the saddest people in the whole world. Maggie and Kate and others like them took advantage of many.

Even today, most priests and rabbis will tell you the same thing. Grieving people are distracted and vulnerable. How can they be sure if they're hearing from the spirit of a dead loved one, or if an evil, or mischievous, spirit is speaking to them through the medium? Also—for the purely practical-minded—how can you *ever* be sure the charming, lovely medium you would love to trust is not tricking you in some way—just like Maggie and Kate Fox tricked their parents (and, eventually, a whole nation!) not so long ago?

Séances in the Bible? "Do not resort to ghosts and spirits or make yourselves unclean by seeking them out," says the book of Leviticus. Pretty strong words! In the book of I Samuel, it's clear that practicing as a medium was illegal. In fact, the penalty was death. Nevertheless, King Saul himself was not able to resist the temptation. When David, the famed defeater of Goliath, was organizing a big army to crush him, Saul put on a disguise and secretly visited a medium—the Witch of Endor—to get advice from the ghost of the departed Samuel. The Witch of Endor was very surprised when she realized who it really was under that cloak. Saul kindly promised he wouldn't have her executed for her services.

How did Maggie and Kate communicate so much just by rapping their toe knuckles? The grown-ups helped them out by working out a code. One rap would mean yes. Silence would mean no. The questioner would hold up an alphabet board and point to letters. When the pointer touched a letter the spirit wanted, it would rap. It was a slow process, but in this way the spirit could spell out whole stories. (Once, Kate's schoolteacher commented wryly that the spirit spelled as badly as Kate did.)

ICKY ECTOPLASM

*Bear in mind, I am not a skeptic. It is my will to believe and if
convincing evidence is brought forward I will be the first to
acknowledge my mistake, but up to the present day nothing has crossed
my path to make me think that the Great Almighty will allow
emanations from a human body of such horrible, revolting, viscous
substances . . . [creating such] hideous shapes, which, like "genii
from the bronze bottle," ring bells, move handkerchiefs, wobble tables,
and do other flap-doodle stunts.* —Harry Houdini

Those who channel words or voices from ghosts
are called spiritual mediums. Kate and Maggie
Fox were spiritual mediums. Once in a while,
their ghostly visitors would wobble tables in their efforts
to communicate with séance sitters, but mostly they just

wanted to talk—rapping or writing secret messages on small chalkboards.

People had heard about poltergeists and how they could rearrange the furniture in a room. Some began to wonder if maybe mediums could channel poltergeist energy, too. It wasn't long after the first spiritual mediums began following in Maggie and Kate's footsteps that people who called themselves physical mediums began to find a brisk business for their talents as well.

The special effects that physical mediums had at their command were sometimes quite dazzling. Daniel Dunglas Home was one of the most famous. He was born in Scotland in 1833—the same year as Maggie Fox. Home said that spirits began talking with him when he was a small child. His aunt said that when he was an infant, she would walk into the nursery, only to find his cradle being rocked by some invisible force. At the tender age of three, he foresaw the death of a young cousin.

By that time, his mom and dad were having a hard time making ends meet. They didn't have the means or the energy to take care of their frail, high-strung little

Daniel, who talked to ghosts. His aunt and uncle agreed to adopt him, and they soon moved to Connecticut. There Daniel and his best friend, Edwin, made a pact that if one of them died, the other would do his best to contact the other. Not long after that, Daniel and his family moved again, and he and Edwin lost touch. Then, when he was thirteen, Daniel had a vivid crisis apparition: one night he saw the figure of his friend, surrounded by a bright glowing aura, standing near the foot of his bed. The misty form of Edwin made three circles in the air and then vanished. Not long after that, Daniel found out that Edwin had died.

Home's mother passed away when he was still a young lad too, and he claimed that he had foreseen her death three days before it happened. She continued to come to him in visions throughout his life—no doubt appearing more often than she had when she was alive.

At the age of eighteen—just a couple of years after Maggie and Kate had hit the headlines—Daniel announced to his aunt that he'd decided to become a Spiritualist medium. She told him that was an evil occupation. Their house soon became haunted by ghostly rappers and furniture movers.

His aunt told him to send the spirits away. When he defied her, she picked up a kitchen chair and flung it at him. (Proving that you don't have to be invisible to move furniture.) If Spiritualism was to be his life's work, she said, she wanted him out of her house forever. Apparently she did not mean *forever*-forever, because later, when he became famous and married a wealthy Russian noblewoman, she relented.

There was something about D. D. Home that made people go gaga over him wherever he went. He was tall, blue-eyed, and handsome, and always a bit thin and sickly looking. People found him very sweet and charming. He never asked for a penny. But he was never without a mansion to stay in, or without fine food and clothes and jewels. People who were reunited with lost loved ones through his séances were all too happy to shower him with expensive gifts.

He had a *particularly* charming way of making emerald bracelets and diamond necklaces dematerialize and then rematerialize on the séance table, right in front of everyone's eyes. He said the spirits liked to play with them. Occasionally a bracelet or two remained in the spirit realm. Oddly, their owners didn't seem to mind. Maybe they thought these light-fingered spirits were the ghosts of annoying friends who, even in life, had been prone to borrowing stuff and forgetting to return it.

Then in 1852 Home did something that got the attention of newspapers all over the country. After a séance, when the spirits had finished rapping their messages to the seated guests, Home left the table, and his body slowly rose up into the air. Up he rose, until his head touched the ceiling. The whole time, the astonished guests heard spirits rapping. And they heard what sounded like the crashing of waves and the creaks of a ship at sea. (Or was it the creaks of pulleys and thin wires lifting him? Maybe. But the witnesses were baffled. They didn't see a thing.)

In his most amazing feat of levitation, Home sailed out a three-story window and floated back in another. Of course none of the witnesses actually saw Home open the first window and sail out. They waited patiently in the next room, as they were told. But, they were predictably aghast when they saw the medium float into their room through the open window.

Newspaper reporters had a field day, and the story was soon accepted as true. Home explained that spirits kept him afloat. Skeptics came up with many possible explanations for Home's mysterious powers. They were able to duplicate some of his tricks, but not all of them.

One of Home's acts was especially creepy and memorable. In the dim light, a pale, ghostly hand would appear— wavering and floating over the séance table, as if reaching out—pushing itself forth, through unknown barriers, from the world beyond, into the world of the living. Home would invite séance sitters to shake the ghost's hand. The ghost would introduce itself as a dear departed friend or relative.

How could a spirit—or part of a spirit—take on physical form? Great minds went to work to figure it out. Meanwhile, mediums began to experiment with even better-looking ghostly hands and legs and faces and . . . What in the world—or out of this world—were these ghostly limbs made of!?

It's sticky, it's icky—it's *ectoplasm*. What's that, you ask? Well, it's stuff. It's a kind of goopy, slimy, slippery stuff that oozes out of a medium's body when a spirit's energy force wants to come from the world beyond into the material world and make itself visible. Got that?

Today everyone knows that our bodies are made up of many different kinds of cells, all working together. If you haven't already, you'll learn about that in your seventh- or eighth-grade biology class. In the early 1800s, you wouldn't have had to memorize any of that information, because it wouldn't have been in your textbook yet.

At that time, scientists were just beginning to understand how cells work. But what was between the cells? What held them all together? People had all kinds of ideas about it. Some Spiritualists suggested that oozy stuff—stuff that is in a state somewhere between the spiritual and the physical—flows between our cells. There really isn't any oozy stuff flowing between your cells, but it got a name anyway: "ectoplasm." The word was coined in 1894 by the

French doctor, Charles Richet. Spiritualists believed that ectoplasm could be activated, squeezed out of the body, and shaped by spiritual forces.

Okay. If you've got a weak stomach or are about to go eat your dinner, stop right here. Don't look! This is one of my favorite photographs of ectoplasm. It was taken at a séance. The photograph shows the medium in a trance with ectoplasm coming out of her ear. (I will be kind and not show you my second favorite—the one where it's coming out of her nose.)

The ectoplasm looks like that foamy string stuff you

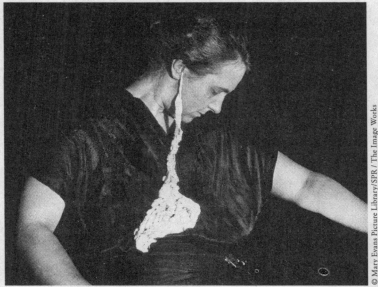

shoot out of a can. But, of course, string stuff you shoot out of a can had not been invented yet. So what on earth was it? Sorry, I don't even want to think about it!

Ectoplasm often took on the shape of pallid hands or even faces of departed loved ones. Medium Florence Cook was the first to produce a glob of ectoplasm that took on a complete human form. Her most famous extrusion was a ghost named Katie King.

Author Mary Roach visited the Cambridge University Library in England, where they keep a hunk of old ectoplasm locked up in the archives. When she unwrapped it, she discovered it to be a piece of satiny white cloth, stained here and there with little brownish spots. The cloth is about ten feet long and three feet wide. This is the "ectoplasm" the medium Helen Duncan let ooze (or appeared to let ooze) from her mouth during a séance around 1939. Roach suspects that Mr. Duncan, who insisted on sitting next to his wife during séances, might have secretly slipped the stuff to her while she distracted the sitters. It is pretty gross to imagine anyone cramming ten feet of cloth into his or her mouth or, even worse, swallowing it all and then regurgitating it (that means barfing it up, in case you don't know) on cue, so I hope she is right.

Slimer is the gross green ghost in the Ghostbuster movies and cartoons. He's green and he's horrible *and* he can spew slime. Slimer plays the character of a bad ghost who has mended his evil ways and joined the Ghostbusters team. If Slimer's slime reminds you a bit of icky ectoplasm, well, it should! Where do you think the idea of a ghost "sliming" a person came from?

In the Ghostbusters comics, the ghost hunters, when threatened by a malevolent spirit, can use the "Ecto-Splat" device to shoot a jet of ectoplasm. Ectoplasm can hit the ghost where it hurts. Ordinary guns would, of course, be useless, since bullets go right through a ghost.

IT'S MAGICAL!

Up to the present time, everything that I have investigated has been the result of deluded brains or those which were too actively and intensely willing to believe. —Harry Houdini

Magic is . . . well—it's magical! I don't know how to perform any magic tricks, but I do know I love a great magic show. Once, when I was a kid, I met a famous magician. As we sat at a table munching on some snack crackers and chatting, he told me to hold out my hand, palm up. I did, and he touched the palm of my hand with his magic wand. Then he told me to turn my hand over and make a fist. Again, I did as I was told. He tapped the top of my hand twice with his wand and told me to turn my hand over and open it up again. I turned my hand over and opened it and . . . there in the palm of my hand was the prettiest little golden ball I'd ever seen. How did he do that? I don't have the slightest idea. But I do know that it was real magic. Sleight of hand. Legerdemain. Prestidigitation. I love those words.

It is possible for a talented magician to completely fool our five senses, no matter how smart and attentive we think we are. The little golden ball was not placed in my hand by a ghost who wanted to get a message to me from the beyond. But—if a very talented and very dishonest magician told his or her audience that the ball contained an important message from a spirit, then at least some of the people in the audience would believe it.

D. D. Home and the Fox sisters convinced prime ministers and emperors, state governors and U.S. senators, presidents of big companies, doctors, social reformers, and even investigative scientists that they were talking to their dead loved ones. How did they do it?

In 1888—forty years after the first rappings in the

Hydesville bedroom—Maggie Fox confessed. She told the world it had all been made up. It was an elaborate trick. Still, many people absolutely refused to believe her. Girls of that time were supposed to be quiet and demure. No one could believe that two sweet, lovely teenagers could have created and sustained such a monumental fraud.

The Fox sisters had a lot of natural talent. They were certainly smart and sensitive and intuitive about other people's feelings. They probably had photographic memories and great manual dexterity. It is amazing what ordinary human beings can do.

The only thing is . . . okay . . . I don't know about you, but I feel an indignant and preachy mood coming over me: each and every one of us should think about how we can apply our unique talents in useful ways and not in fooling people and wasting their time and energy. Really!

Maggie realized this. But when she finally told the truth, millions of people ignored her confession, and thousands of other mediums went on tricking people. Maybe her lies were so attractive, people were happier believing them. A few of the mediums who followed in her footsteps might have been sincere in their belief that they could channel ghosts. But those who were not deliberately fooling others were probably fooling themselves. Were the cleverest, most successful mediums using magic to create their effects? Harry Houdini suspected so. But could he prove it?

Harry Houdini was born in 1874, and he began studying magic when he was twelve years old. In later life, Houdini blossomed into one of the greatest magicians and escape artists the world has ever seen. With his intense gray eyes and charming smile, no one who saw him perform ever forgot it. And the things he could do! Any good magician can make an emerald bracelet disappear. Houdini could make a five-thousand-pound elephant vanish. Even the elephant, he said, didn't know how it was done. He challenged the most experienced jailers in the world to shackle his legs, handcuff his arms, tie him with ropes, and lock him up in their strongest top-security cells. Within minutes he would be sauntering free, flashing his death-defying smile and waving for the astonished crowds.

When he and his wife, Bess, were young, though, they had a tough time making a living. Jobs at circuses and magic shows were few and far between. When they did get gigs, they didn't pay very well, and they were often way out in the boondocks. One summer they traveled all around Kansas with a medicine show. (I'm sorry if you are from Kansas. But this was 1897 and Kansas was the boondocks back then.) Harry and Bess would get people's attention with their magic tricks, and then the two quack "doctors" who ran the show would sell their tonics and magic elixirs to the gathering crowd. When the show went bust in Galena, Houdini had an idea how to save it. Spiritualism was all the rage. How about if they staged a séance? The quacks loved the idea. They put up signs inviting the public to a séance led by the "Great Houdini" at the Opera House that Sunday night. They promised everyone, "Ghosts Will Walk!"

That morning Houdini wandered the local graveyard, boning up on the dead. He remembered everyone's names and when they died and what people said about them on their tombstones. Then he figured out who was the biggest gossip in town and hung out with him for a while. He paid the man a few dollars not to mention their conversation.

The Sunday-night séance was a huge hit. It was clear to Houdini that this was where the money was, and he promptly added ghost wrangling to his show.

But not for long. After a few weeks he began to feel bad about the whole thing. It was so easy, it was pathetic. How could he live with himself, making money off the griefs and sorrows of others? Fooling them into thinking they were talking to their dead loved ones!? It was too horrible. Money or no money, he just couldn't do it. Houdini concentrated on perfecting his great escapes and put ghosts and spirits out of his mind.

Then, when he was in his early forties, he lost his beloved mother. He had always been a religious man, and he said that he believed her soul was in Heaven. Every now and then he felt sure she was looking after him in some mysterious, inexplicable way. But, he wondered— were there mediums out there who could help him have a genuine conversation with her? No one on earth, he said, could wish to have a few words with a departed loved one more than he wished for a few words with his mom. His short run as a medium made him suspicious of others who made their living that way. But he wanted to give it a try. In order to believe the extraordinary claim that a medium could channel his mother's, or anybody else's, ghost, he would need extraordinary proof. If the mediums were using magic tricks, he figured he would spot them. If they were genuine . . . well, he was willing to believe.

In his attempt to contact his mother, Houdini went to hundreds of séances. He came away very disappointed. He believed that in every single séance, the mediums were using tricks to fool him and the other sitters.

Have you ever read any of the Sherlock Holmes stories? If you haven't, you should. Sherlock Holmes is a great detective who solves crimes by carefully observing and analyzing all the clues and making smart conclusions based on the facts. The stories were written by Sir Arthur Conan Doyle. Doyle was a big, lovable guy. He lived in Great Britain with his beautiful wife and five adoring children. Everyone who met him admired his strength and fairness. Doyle and Houdini were good friends, but they started to quarrel over one thing: ghosts!

Doyle told Houdini that he realized a few mediums

might be dishonest, but that didn't mean they all were. Doyle had lost a brave son in World War I, and he became hooked on séances, where he believed he could talk to the young man's spirit. He told Houdini that if he wanted to reach his mother, he should be more open-minded and keep trying.

Houdini told Doyle he was being foolish and gullible. "I am a *magician,* and I know all the tricks!" he shouted. "They are tricking you! You should listen to me. I am your friend!"

Doyle, the creator of Sherlock Holmes, the world's greatest detective, was indignant. He told Houdini he suspected he was using the assistance of spirits in his magic acts and in his great escapes. He said he thought Houdini was trying to hide the fact that spirits helped him and to unjustly take credit for all the magic himself.

Houdini shot back that while what he did was certainly difficult, not one bit of it was supernatural. "My methods are perfectly natural," he cried, "resting on natural laws of physics. . . . I simply control and manipulate material things in a manner . . . equally understandable (if not duplicable) by any person to whom I may elect to divulge my secrets!"

Like many scientists of the day, Doyle considered mediumship a scientific pursuit too. As far as he was concerned, it provided solid evidence—real, material clues—from the world beyond (or "Summerland" as Spiritualists called it). Maybe, he said, Houdini was just a little too prideful to see that.

Houdini didn't think so. In 1923, he and a handful of scientists and distinguished professors from Harvard and MIT posted a challenge in *Scientific American* magazine. They offered a $5,000 prize for any medium who could bring on "ghost communications"—voices, tappings, writings, tipping tables, ringing bells, ectoplasmic excretions, you name it—that Harry Houdini could not duplicate using only his talents as a magician, with no help from spirits of any kind.

During a vacation in America with his wife and children, Sir Arthur Conan Doyle met Mina Crandon, who had already begun to make a name for herself as the medium "Margery." With her sparkling blue eyes and fashionable blonde bob, she soon became one of Doyle's favorite mediums. He thought her oozing ectoplasm was the solid proof that would finally show Houdini he was wrong. Doyle recommended that the *Scientific American* committee attend some of her séances.

Margery must have been very convincing, because in 1924, the committee was coming to the conclusion that Margery was genuine. They had observed her séances with close attention and with what they thought were excellent controls to keep her honest. She must be the real deal, they thought. A true ghost talker! They told the very-busy Houdini that they were con-sidering awarding her the $5,000 prize. Although, of course, they wanted to confer with him first.

Houdini was furious! Why had they waited so long to call him in? "She's a shallow, vampish, flimflam artist!" he cried, reading over their reports. His hot temper showed when he knew he was right about something. He thought maybe his sweet friend Doyle's brain turned to mush around Margery because she was so pretty. But what on earth had made the *Scientific American* committee believe her? Houdini was determined to find out.

Houdini rushed to Boston where she lived, and they scheduled a séance. The sitters gathered at the table, and Houdini sat next to Margery, on her left-hand side. Her husband sat to her right. In order to prove that she was not moving her hands and feet, everyone joined hands. Then Houdini placed his right foot beside her left foot, pressing his ankle against hers. The lights were dimmed.

As usual, Margery went into her trance and invoked the ghost of her dead brother, Walter. Walter would signal his arrival in the room by ringing an electric bell. Naturally, the committee investigators thought Margery might simply ring the bell herself, using some manner of sleight of hand. So, they had the bell locked up in a wooden box. They would set it in the middle of the table. To set off the bell would mean that you had to reach out and press the boards that covered the top of the box. With everyone firmly holding hands—especially hers—there would be no way for her to reach the bell to ring it herself. Of course, the bell rang. No matter what they did to restrain Margery, the bell rang. The scientists were baffled. Could it truly be the ghost? They had no other explanation.

Now Houdini took matters into his own hands. Or into his own feet, really! He insisted that this time the box with the bell be placed between his feet. For several hours before the séance, Houdini wore a tight rubber strap around his leg, just below his knee. By the time the séance began, his leg was ultrasensitive. He also rolled up his pant leg. He would be able to feel it if Margery made even the slightest movement with her foot. As the séance progressed, Houdini could feel Margery's ankle slowly sliding . . . inching ever so slowly upward. She was raising her foot up out of her shoe, to touch the top of the box. When she finally had her foot in position, he could feel the tendons in her leg moving in time with the ringing of the bell.

After the séance was over and Houdini was alone with the other committee members, he declared, "I've got her.

All fraud!" He wrote up a description of the bell trick and many of her other tricks, which he was able to figure out. Doyle was mad at Houdini for exposing Margery. He said Houdini was mean and unfair. In spite of Houdini's detailed explanation of her fraud, many stuck by her, remaining true believers.

Doyle was a very generous, trusting person. But most scientists considered themselves hard-bitten skeptics. Besides the folks on the *Scientific American* committee, several other scientists took it upon themselves to investigate the claims of other popular mediums.

The well-known British scientist, Sir William Crookes, investigated Florence Cook, Daniel Dunglas Home, and a few others. Crookes was a chemist and physicist who did experiments with electricity and discovered cathode rays. That eventually led to the creation of the cathode ray tube, which was an important step toward creating the first televisions. So, if you're tempted to make fun of him for being fooled—take heed! He was a smart guy—maybe just a little too vulnerable and willing to believe. Like many at that time, he had lost a beloved brother to yellow fever, and his grief over the loss was almost unbearable.

Like other scientific investigators of his time, he took extreme measures to try to prevent any hanky-panky on the medium's part. All the medium's orifices (if you don't know what an orifice is, you can go look it up!) would be checked ahead of time. The medium would be tied up with ropes and taped to the chair with duct tape so she or he could barely move. The investigator's assistants would hold the medium's hands and feet. Women wore voluminous skirts back then. So, sometimes a female medium (the majority of mediums were female) would be dressed in a tight-fitting leotard, to prove she was not hiding fake spirit props under her clothing.

Crookes took photographs of Cook with her spirit guide, Katie King, and of others with their somewhat less sophisticated ectoplasmic manifestations. Why didn't he just grab some of that ectoplasm and put it to chemical analysis? He was a chemist, after all! Maybe it's because he was taught to be polite with young women. Or maybe he was afraid of harming the spirits or the medium (or of totally grossing himself out by touching it?). Ectoplasm always had a mysterious way of vanishing before the end of the séance.

Crookes also took photos of D. D. Home levitating. He remained convinced of the truthfulness of most mediums he tested, but his photographs later became some of the best evidence for ghost debunkers. Why Crookes, and many other scientists, were blind to the fraud is a puzzling question.

This is what really troubled Harry Houdini: that not just average people, but also plenty of extremely well-educated people were taken in by mediums. It's not surprising that some scientists were interested in Spiritualism. If the mediums—even just a few—were honest, and if they were correct that their disembodied sounds and table tippings and ectoplasmic hands came from the spirit world, it meant that for the first time, there might be real, tangible proof of the immortality of the soul. Scientists love tangible proof. But before they can allow themselves to believe, they must first put their observations to the test. So, these scientists created what they thought were completely controlled situations, where any tricks the mediums might be tempted to play would be impossible.

Still, they were fooled. Houdini felt sorry for these otherwise smart scientists. And he didn't want them to discredit themselves. He knew his own training in the art of magic gave him a better chance of figuring out exactly how the mediums were tricking people. He made it his mission to explain those tricks in his books and pamphlets and lectures. Many magicians today, like James Randi and Penn and Teller, carry on with Houdini's work, explaining the tricks people try to pass off as supernatural.

Courtesy of the Library of Congress

When Houdini was investigating a medium, he sometimes locked the medium in this box to assure that he or she would not be able to play any tricks during the séance.

A book called *Hocus Pocus; or, The Whole Art of Conjuring Made Easy for Young Persons* was a popular kids' book when Maggie and Kate Fox were growing up.

Kate Fox dabbled in slate writing, but "Dr." Henry Slade was the real expert. He had a small slate board that could be covered and locked shut. During a séance, he would lock up the blank slate, ask the attending spirit a question, then open the slate and . . . voilà! The spirit's answer would be there, written in chalk on the slate. The trick baffled many investigators. But his fraud was finally exposed, and he nearly ended up in jail.

SMILE AND SAY "BOO!"

I have never been in any humbug business where I did not give value for the money. —Phineas T. Barnum

While exposing the tricks used at séances, Harry Houdini also took on the booming business of spirit photography. Photographs of ghosts? How could anyone believe in that? you ask. Well, today you can take a photo with your cell phone and send it to your grandmother across the country in less than a second. But take a second to think back to the 1800s. The very first photographs ever taken were produced around 1822. It was a slow and painstaking process, and only a few experts even tried it.

In 1839 the French chemist Louis Daguerre invented a simpler process for making photographs. Pictures taken by his method were called daguerreotypes. Still, this method required expensive silver plates for picking up the photographic images. For a long time, only professional photographers took pictures. Most people didn't have the time or the money for it.

Flaws in the silver plates, accidents during the developing process, or an odd source of light that the photographer overlooked while taking the picture could all cause weird images or baffling effects in the photo. Some photographers honestly thought (and hoped!) they had captured ghosts on silver plates and, later, on film. But most figured out how these things happened and learned how to get better control of the end results. After all, they wanted to make the clearest photos possible.

Sometime in the 1860s, though, when photography was still a mysterious process to most people, spirit photography became a big business. These photographers knew exactly what they were doing. And, sad to say, their market was huge. Over 600,000 young people lost their lives during the American Civil War. Most of these soldiers died far from home. Families who had lost loved ones hoped beyond hope that they might see their faces just one last time.

Photographers like William Mumler told them they could help. Mumler would invite a grieving person into his studio to have his portrait taken. If everything was done reverently and just right, he said, the portrait might reveal the ghost of the departed loved one. Of course it would be expensive to make sure everything was "just right." The bereaved were willing to pay almost any price. And Mumler attracted the wealthiest clients. After President Abraham Lincoln was assassinated in the Ford Theatre in 1865, Mary Todd Lincoln went to Mumler for an afterlife family portrait. (She said that she hid her true identity from Mumler. But it's hard to believe he did not recognize the First Lady.) Miraculously, Mumler seemed to have captured the ghost of Abe looming, warm and kindly, over the grieving widow.

Before Houdini was even born, the great circus director

Phineas T. Barnum was outraged by these so-called spirit photos. Barnum devoted a lot of time to uncovering hoaxes. But the photographers who created and sold spirit photos, he said, were hoaxers of the most despicable kind. They were taking terrible advantage of grieving families.

In 1869, when William Mumler was finally put on trial for fraud, Barnum asked a photographer to take a photo of him and make it look as if the ghost of Abraham Lincoln was watching over him. He showed this photo as evidence in the trial and explained to the jury how it had been done. A well-known Supreme Court judge, who happened to be a Spiritualist, testified in Mumler's favor. And Mumler's lawyer took a jab at Barnum, saying he was no slouch at fooling people himself! Barnum said that the difference between him and the photo hoaxers was that his creations were made to entertain people and to make them laugh and think, not to take advantage of their sorrow and their faith. In spite of Barnum's testimony, Mumler was found not guilty.

Enraged, Barnum bought some of Mumler's photos and hung them in his museum in New York City. Underneath, in big letters, he posted the label, "Spiritualistic Humbugs."

After the trial, Mumler quietly faded into the woodwork. I guess he decided to quit while he was ahead. But the trial didn't stop others from following in his footsteps.

Much to Houdini's dismay, people were still being fooled by spirit photographers well into the twentieth century. Photographer William Hope was one of the worst offenders. Houdini suspected that Mr. Hope provided not hope but only delusion. In the 1920s Hope organized a group of photographers in his hometown of Crewe, England. They called themselves the Crewe Circle. They claimed to have captured on film more than two thousand five hundred "ghost extras." They would start their portrait sessions with prayers and hymns. Many devout people flocked to the Circle to have their portraits taken with dead relatives.

These photographers had been able to create some of their hoax photos even while skeptical investigators were watching them. But, as with Barnum, very little could escape Houdini's keen senses, trained as he was in the art of magic. Houdini tried to schedule a portrait session with Hope. Hope fumbled with his appointment calendar and told him he was busy for months and months and months—maybe even years! He told Houdini he would just have to wait. So Houdini called a good friend of his, who was also a magician. He asked his friend to make an appointment with Hope. A few days later Houdini's friend was sitting for his portrait.

After the sitting, Houdini and his friend were able to write a detailed explanation of how Hope's photos with "ghost extras" were made. The Crewe Circle used the simple process of double exposure, that is, taking a fuzzy photo of a person (or sometimes even of a doll!) and then using the same film or plate to take the photo of the hopeful bereaved. Houdini's friend explained how plates that Hope had already exposed were exchanged with the sitter's fresh plates by sleight of hand.

Houdini's friend became particularly suspicious at one point when Hope briefly put the palm of his hand in front of the camera's lens while a photo was being taken. An odd thing for a photographer to do! The Crewe Circle's photos often included weird "spirit lights." These effects, Houdini's friend deduced, were created by special luminescent chemicals that the photographer had rubbed into the palm of his hand.

After months of earnest, open-minded observation of mediums and spirit photographers—hoping to find some true sign that spirits were trying to communicate with the living—Houdini was thoroughly disillusioned. Maybe there are spirit photographers and mediums out there who can sometimes honestly get in touch with ghosts. But no one *ever* won the *Scientific American* prize!

It may be hard for us to believe that photos like this one actually fooled people. But today most of us know a whole lot more about the process of photography than the average person did at that time.

When putting on plays, stage designers sometimes have to produce ghosts. The more convincing, the better! In the 1870s, they could make a ghost appear onstage using Pepper's Illusion. Dr. Pepper figured out how to put a ghost onstage using a large, angled sheet of glass and a light projector. (No, he did not also invent the soda pop of the same name. I checked.) Famous ghosts of drama, such as the ghost of Hamlet's father, became more ghostly looking than ever. Like stage designers, skilled magicians knew how to use light, smoke, and mirrors to create ghostly effects for their audiences. Pepper's Illusion is still used today for haunted-house effects in some of the world's most famous theme parks.

Today photographers with digital cameras have captured "orbs" and other strange light effects that some have claimed are ghosts or signals from spirit entities. What do you think?

Cameras can be useful for ghost investigators, to help them detect the real causes of mysterious phenomena.

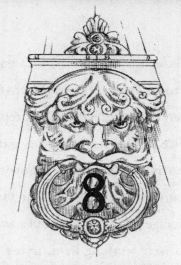

GHOST GADGETS

You see, the Wire Telegraph is a kind of a very, very long cat.
You pull his tail in New York and his head is meowing in Los Angeles.
Do you understand this? And Radio operates exactly the same way:
you send signals here, they receive them there.
The only difference is that there is no cat. —Albert Einstein

Imagine it's 1836 and your best friend has just moved to another town one hundred miles away. You miss him and want to stay in touch. So, you take out your quill pen and ink pot, scribble a letter on a piece of parchment, fold it up and seal it in an envelope, put your friend's name and new address on it, and walk to the post office with it. A postman driving a horse-drawn stagecoach will carry the letter the 100 miles, and your friend will be very excited to get it. He'll open the envelope and read your letter. Then he'll scribble down a reply for you, go to his post office, and send his letter out on the next stagecoach. . . . And *that* is as fast as anyone could communicate with anyone else who lived far away.

While the average person of the 1800s was busy writing letters, scientists were working hard, trying to understand the properties of electricity and magnetism and figuring out ways to produce electrical energy and put it to use.

In 1837 Samuel Morse put electricity and magnetism to use in a most astonishing new way. He created the first telegraph in America. With his first devices, connected by wires, he was able to send messages—in seconds—across a distance of a few miles. It took people a while to get it through their heads how useful this invention could be. But within a decade, telegraph wires connected big cities. By 1861 the wires were strung all the way across the country.

If you wanted to tell your best friend how the bully at school had finally gotten detention or how you got an A on your science project, you'd still write that to him in a letter.

But if his grandma got sick or if a long-lost uncle arrived with a million dollars for him, you did not need to wait for a stagecoach to deliver the news. He could get an urgent message to you within seconds—even across vast lonely stretches of land. The moment you had his message, you could reply in a matter of seconds as well. To most people, it seemed as if this dazzling change in our ability to communicate with each other happened practically overnight.

The telegraph sent a code of short and long raps (the Morse Code) that could be translated into letters of the alphabet. Sound familiar? I suppose no one can say for sure, but I imagine that Kate and Maggie Fox were fascinated by Morse's wonderful new invention. Certainly their big sister, Leah, knew all about the telegraph. In fact, she said it was the ghost of Benjamin Franklin—the Father of Electricity himself—who recommended they use the tappings of the telegraph as their model for the clearest possible spirit communications. In a séance message received by both Kate and Maggie in different places at the same time, the spirit of Franklin declared, "Now I am ready, my friends. There will be great changes in the nineteenth century. Things that now look dark and mysterious to you will be laid plain before your sight. Mysteries are going to be revealed. The world will be enlightened. I sign my name Benjamin Franklin."

The ghostly Ben seemed to promise that the world would be enlightened by the arrival of long-distance communication between Heaven and Earth. Well, the world *was* soon enlightened, but not in the way Leah's Ben predicted.

In 1848, when Leah was holding her first séances, homes were lighted by oil lamps, kids washed dishes in water heated on a woodstove, and if you wanted to talk to someone, you went to visit. Then, in 1879, Thomas Edison created America's first lightbulb. Within a few decades, people would have electric lights, electric stoves, and all kinds of useful appliances in their homes. Alexander Graham Bell patented the telephone in 1876. Much to everyone's amazement, not only raps and taps but actual human voices could be sent, via electricity, through wires. "Great changes" indeed! But could any of these wonderful new inventions help people get in touch with ghosts?

Thomas Edison's parents had been Spiritualists, and he

hoped that a special telephone might one day be invented that would connect the living with the dead. In October 1920, he announced in *Scientific American* magazine that he was working on just that. He said he thought it might be possible to construct a device "so delicate that if there are personalities in another existence who wish to get in touch with us . . . this apparatus will at least give them a better opportunity."

Alas, Edison never created his ghost phone. But others kept trying. Inventors puttered around with gadgets that they hoped might provide reliable means to help spirits get in touch. The new machines would cast away all doubt. Gone would be the dim, mysterious séance rooms, where mediums' accomplices could be sneaking around with props. Now there would be light! A human medium could play tricks on you. But a machine can't play tricks—it always operates in exactly the same way. How great it would be to discover a spirit machine—a reliable, direct line to Heaven!

Some thought radio waves might provide the key. Radio waves were discovered in 1888, and in the 1890s Nikola

Courtesy of the Library of Congress

Tesla and Guglielmo Marconi figured out how to use them to communicate over long distances. On Christmas Eve 1906, Reginald Fessenden made the first radio broadcast. He sent his broadcast from Brant Rock, Massachusetts. Telegraph operators on ships at sea stared at their receivers in disbelief. Instead of the clickety-clack of Morse Code, they were suddenly hearing a disembodied voice reading a passage from the Bible. They could hardly believe their ears. No more would they need to decipher coded raps. Now voices could travel anywhere—wirelessly!

Wires or no wires, hardly anyone understood the science behind these devices. But they changed people's lives dramatically. Many suspected there was something supernatural about them. If electromagnetic radio waves could carry information over great distances, even through vast stretches of empty space, certainly spirits could somehow talk to us from Heaven. Right?

I like Albert Einstein's funny explanation of telegraph and radio, because *that* is how much most people knew about these things at the time. Even the greatest genius of the twentieth century could express how mind-boggling it was for people when they first realized instantaneous long-distance communication was possible. Today we take radio and television broadcasts for granted. We talk to each other all the time on wireless phones. Even though wireless communication has become routine, some people still hope that ghosts might someday join us in the chat room.

Could it happen? Electromagnetic waves can carry

information. Do you understand how this happens? Of course you don't! But you will. When you get to eleventh or twelfth grade, you'll study physics. There is absolutely nothing supernatural about radio and television. Radio waves are very obedient. They obey the laws of physics. Wherever you are in the universe and whoever you are in the world, you can manipulate electromagnetic waves in certain predictable ways to send information or your voice across great distances. Wonderful as this is for us, radio waves don't work for ghosts.

Every time a new or better communications device is invented, there are people who will try to contact spirits with it. Some people have said that ghosts can talk to them through their computers. It's been said that maybe ghosts lurk in the Internet, waiting for an opportunity to make their voices heard. But this kind of idea is not much different from the old-fashioned thinking that photographs could capture the images of your dead loved ones or that Great-Grandma might phone you from Heaven.

Maybe a machine can't play tricks by itself, but sophisticated mediums knew how to employ new gadgets to good effect. Houdini had fun with a "talking teakettle." The science is simple, but most people didn't have a clue what was going on. The medium's secret assistant would sit in the next room and whisper into a transmitter. An induction coil built into the base of the kettle would pick up the broadcast and direct it into a telephone amplifier that had been built into the spout.

In the 1960s Konstantine Raudive thought he might be able to record ghost voices on magnetic tape. Raudive would set up a tape recorder and record . . . nothing—an absolutely silent room. Once in a while,

CONTINUED ON P. 106

105

mysterious voices, which were not heard during the taping process, would be caught on the tape. He called these EVP, or electronic voice phenomena.

You know that crackly static sound you hear on your radio when you have the tuner set between stations? Raudive spent hours taping that, too. When he played the tapes back, he would hear mysterious voices on them. Voices that sometimes called him by name.

No, he wasn't crazy. He certainly heard something in the static, but was it ghosts? He may have been picking up bits of broadcasts from stations far away. Also, people often hear what seem like messages embedded in fuzzy, random sounds—just the way we sometimes see figures in clouds or the face of a departed loved one in a double-exposure photo of a doll.

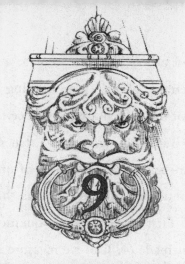

HOW MUCH DOES A GHOST WEIGH?

How can I possibly prove it doesn't *exist? . . . I mean, you could claim that* anything's *real if the only basis for believing in it is that nobody's proved it doesn't exist.* —Hermione, *HARRY POTTER AND THE DEATHLY HALLOWS*

It's time for the annual science fair at your school, and you have a brilliant idea. You're going to try to weigh and measure the human soul. You get out your notebook and pencils and start to devise an experiment. . . .

Well, you're not going to win any popularity contests with your science teachers with that idea, I'll tell you that right now.

Houdini and others like him went to a lot of trouble proving that certain "ghosts" were nothing but tricks and illusions. It's not too difficult to prove a certain something is *not* a ghost. But can anyone prove that something *is* a ghost? There are scientists at a couple of universities who are trying to come up with experiments that will give us concrete proof. First of all, they ask questions: What is a soul? What is it made of? Can we measure it? Can we see it—or detect it in some way—as it departs from a dead body?

Then, of course, they have to think of reliable ways to answer those questions. That's the really hard (some might even say impossible!) part.

You could start your science-fair project by describing the 1907 experiments of Duncan Macdougall. In your list of materials, include a very large scale and a bunch of people who are about to die any second.

Dr. Macdougall believed that the soul leaves the body as soon as a person dies. He figured that the soul must have some weight. So, if you could somehow get a dying person on a scale and then watch his weight, you would see him suddenly become lighter right at the moment of his death. Whatever weight he lost when he died would be the weight of his soul.

Where do you go to find lots of people willing to die on a scale? Dr. Macdougall set up his soul-weighing lab in a sanatorium in Haverhill, Massachusetts. A sanatorium was a type of hospital where doctors used to send people who were dying of diseases such as tuberculosis. Today we use powerful antibiotics to help cure tuberculosis. There was no cure back then.

Six patients agreed to help Macdougall with his experiment. Two of the experiments were goofed up. (One of the patients inconveniently died before the doctor could get the scale properly adjusted!) The four that went smoothly did show some weight loss at the time of death. The loss varied from person to person, but Macdougall recorded it at somewhere between one half an ounce and an ounce and a quarter.

When I imagine Dr. Macdougall in his lab, I can't help seeing Gene Wilder as "Young Frankenstein," shouting, "Alive! It's alive!" as his monster's eyes pop open for the

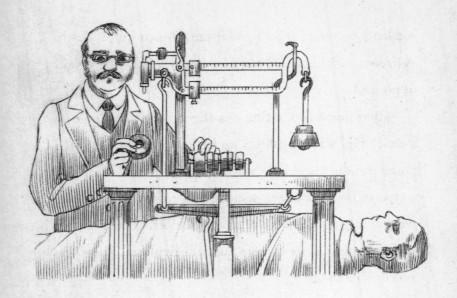

first time. Except in this version, the mad scientist is shouting, "Dead! He's dead!" while keeping his eyes glued to the quivering bar on his scale.

Macdougall repeated his experiment with fifteen dogs. He did not believe dogs had souls. As expected, he didn't see any loss of weight at the time of the dogs' deaths. Macdougall believed this proved his experiments had been a success.

He published the results of his experiments in the journal *American Medicine*. Most scientists who read about the experiments groaned in dismay. They complained that his sample size was way too small. His scale was not all that precise. And how could he be sure exactly what had caused the peoples' weight loss?

And, I might add, who's to say that dogs don't have souls, eh?

At the conclusion of your description, be sure to add a banner saying, "This is an example of how *not* to do a science experiment." You will have to do a better job of designing yours.

Throughout history, every time a new invention or discovery hit the headlines, it opened the possibility that this might finally give us a way to perceive the human soul or a means to get in touch with departed loved ones. The ectoplasm craze developed around the time scientists were making new discoveries in biology. The spirit photo craze took root after the discovery of photography. Throughout the twentieth century and on into our own, new ideas and inventions have been making observations of previously invisible forces, waves, and particles possible. Will we be able to use some of these devices to see the soul?

In spite of the fancy gadgets you see put to use on shows on the Syfy Channel, no one has come up with a departing (or incoming) soul detector. Some scientists have devised interesting experiments. But so far, no one else has been able to repeat those experiments and get the same, or similar, results. An experiment that cannot be successfully repeated by others is a big zero—a flop—a failure.

Perhaps a few scientists will go on coming up with hypotheses about the soul and trying to devise experiments to test them. Most scientists would much rather study easier questions, though. Questions that have way better chances of being successfully answered—like how to cure a certain disease, or if there was once life on Mars. Chances are excellent that scientists will figure things like this out.

When it comes to questions like "What happens to the soul when we die?" or "Can the soul of a dead person appear to the living?" . . . well, perhaps it's misguided or just plain wrong for Macdougall or any scientist to think that the soul is made of some natural substance that can be weighed or measured. Maybe the soul is entirely supernatural. Who knows? Maybe someday someone will devise an experiment that will tell us once and for all what the soul is made of. But until then, the way we answer questions like these will remain a matter of faith.

One question we might be able to answer is why many people firmly believe they have seen or interacted with ghosts. One explanation is because they *have* seen them. A better explanation, says expert ghost detective Benjamin Radford, is that "people misunderstand and misperceive things all the time; it doesn't mean that they are stupid or crazy, just that they do not necessarily know what to look for."

Way back in 1848, Mrs. Fox believed she was hearing ghosts. The raps were perfectly ordinary noises. But to her, they were unfamiliar and strange. She began to imagine what might be causing the strange sounds. Without any direct evidence, there could be any number of possible answers. She happened to seize upon the answer that the raps were made by ghosts. After that, everything she saw and heard and felt just served to reinforce her conclusion, even though it was completely wrong.

People everywhere do this every day. Every day we are

faced with puzzles and mysteries. Whenever we are, we almost immediately begin to make up answers to explain them. Some of those answers are going to be correct, others will be wrong. How do you tell if an idea is right or wrong? Well you've got to test it. Try it out. Instead of only looking for proof that your idea is right, try to prove that it's wrong.

If you're uncertain about something, that's okay too. To declare you don't know for sure is better than to be certain you're right about an answer that's wrong. Part of being human is to explore mysteries and to look for answers. If we want to thrive, we have to make sure that most of the time we get the right answers.

Is that dark, gloomy house down the wooded lane haunted? What are those strange creaking sounds I hear out in the hall at night? Think about all the possibilities and look closely at all the evidence. Most of the time you will find the answers—and you will be right.

Sometimes you will have harder questions that can't be answered so easily. What was that strange vision I experienced? I saw my friend in trouble—only to find out later that he actually had been in trouble. Or, I was in trouble, but I felt my grandfather's ghost watching over me, and I knew what to do. What causes these weird, otherworldly perceptions?

Whatever they are, people will go on "experiencing apparitions" as long as humans are human. And great ghost stories will still keep us glued to our seats as we wonder, What is out there in the mysterious world beyond? Someday, maybe we will know for sure.

Meanwhile, remember—there will always be a few people who would love to benefit from tricking you. We have to thank honest magicians and circus entertainers like Phineas T. Barnum who help us stay sharp. They poke fun at us a little and remind us how easily we can be fooled. They keep us thinking.

If you go to the Barnum Museum in Bridgeport, Connecticut, you'll see a sign Barnum was fond of using in his circus shows. It reads, THIS WAY TO THE EGRESS!—25¢. Excited by the prospect of seeing an egress, whatever that was, willing crowds paid their quarters and lined up. Slowly they made their way through a long, dark canvas tent tunnel and out a doorway. When they emerged, they found themselves blinking in the sunlight on an empty street corner. Invariably people would storm back to the entrance of the big top. They'd demand to be let back in. The ticket seller would just smile and say, "Sure, that'll be twenty-five cents, please."

Outraged, the people would shout, "I already paid admission!" And the ticket seller would calmly say, "But you're here. Anyone who wants to go in has to pay admission." Some understood right away. They'd been had! They laughed at the joke and handed over their quarters. Others grumbled indignantly. P. T. Barnum said to the indignant grumblers of this world, "You pay me to fool you. This is what I do. This is why you like my great circus. Egress is just another word for exit. It's not some exotic animal or foreign princess. You should know that, you dummies!" After that, even the grumblers were laughing. Although a bit ruefully!

So, don't grumble, and remember to laugh a little every day. Most of all, always pay attention and ask questions. If people try to make fun of your questions, push harder—ask again. And keep thinking! Keep exploring! You may never discover a reliable way to talk to ghosts, or a device that can weigh and measure the soul, but don't fret—I guarantee that you will find out some amazing things. This world is full of more wonders—*real* wonders—than are dreamed of, even in your wildest, craziest imaginings.

AUTHOR'S NOTE

I grew up in the Catskill Mountains, in upstate New York—a place made famous by some of Washington Irving's spooky stories. My mom, dad, and I lived in a farmhouse built by Dutch settlers in 1784. Those settlers were my distant relatives, and relatives of mine have lived in that house ever since. When I was growing up, we liked to imagine that one of those old relatives was haunting the place. Day or night we would hear mysterious creaks or knocking sounds. While playing cards at the dining-room table, we'd occasionally hear footsteps on the stairs. The door to the stairwell would swing open of its own accord. "That's just Uncle George," my dad would say to frightened guests.

That always made me giggle. As far as I knew, there'd never been any "Uncle George" in the family. There were probably ordinary explanations for the noises and swinging doors. Temperature changes can make parts of an old house expand or contract at different rates, causing odd creaks and thumps. Drafts from cracked or open windows can make doors swing open or slam shut. But it was a thrill to think there might be a ghost behind it all.

Sometimes the water faucets in the kitchen would turn themselves on, full bore. "Uncle George," was my father's explanation. That was much funnier than my mom's more practical suggestion that perhaps the faucets needed new washers!

At times that strange uncle could really get me in trouble. Once, when I was in bed for my nap (kids had to take naps in those days), my mom, downstairs in the kitchen, heard what sounded like an acrobat on a trampoline overhead. She yelled upstairs, telling me to stop jumping on the bed and get to sleep. Naptime was not over! But I *was* sleeping. *Really*—I was! "It was Uncle George!" I cried. Later we heard that there'd been a mild earthquake in our area at that time.

Only once, when my doorknob rattled and shook in the middle of the night, did I ever feel frightened of the ghost. I sprang out of bed and peeked out the door. No one was there. Maybe it was just a vivid dream. I preferred to think it was Uncle George—that mysterious old relative who wouldn't leave.

There was no history of violence in our house; no skeletons buried in the cellar! The house sits on a lovely hill, with a nice view of the mountains all around. My mother claims it's the prettiest spot in the world. So maybe it's no wonder Uncle George, whoever he was, wanted to hang around for a little longer than his allotted time on this earth. Maybe he was just an incurable old prankster, and that night he wanted to wake me up to see the beautiful star-lit sky.

My parents still live in the same house in the Catskills, but they have not had any Uncle George sightings in many years. I like to imagine that his ghost is at rest now. I hope he has gone on to an even prettier place. Do I believe in ghosts? Well, I would like to, but I have not found enough evidence. Not *yet* anyway!

CHECK OUT SOME OTHER GHOSTLY BOOKS FROM ALADDIN:

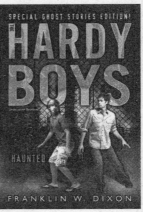